SETTLERS AND STRANGERS

SETTLERS AND STRANGERS

NATIVE AMERICANS OF THE DESERT SOUTHWEST AND HISTORY AS THEY SAW IT

by Betty Baker

MACMILLAN PUBLISHING CO., INC.
NEW YORK

Picture Credits: Arizona Historical Society, 54, 64, 69; Arizona State Museum, title page, 25, 40; Arizona State Museum (E. W. Haury), 45 bottom, 49; Arizona State Museum (E. B. Sayles), 30 bottom, 83; Arizona State Museum (Helga Teiwes), 8, 10, 14, 30 top left, 36, 39, 41, 81; The Bettmann Archive, Inc., 45 top, 52, 63, 66, 77; The Heard Museum, Phoenix (Abrams Photo/Graphics), 29; Historical Pictures Service, Inc., Chicago, 43, 67, 68; Mesa Verde National Park, 11, 13, 20, 21; Museum of the American Indian, Heye Foundation, 18, 30 top right, 34; The National Archives, 6 (D. Griffiths, Bureau of Agricultural Economics), 74 (Office of the Chief of Engineers), 71 (U.S. Signal Corps); National Park Service, U.S. Department of the Interior (Fred E. Mang, Jr.), 23, 32; Smithsonian Institution in The National Archives, 61, 78 (A. J. McDonald), 80; Smithsonian Institution National Anthropological Archives, Bureau of American Ethnology Collection, 72 (G. Wharton James), 82 (James Mooney).

Macmillan Publishing Co., Inc.
866 Third Avenue, New York, N.Y. 10022
Collier Macmillan Canada, Ltd.

Designed by Bobye List/Map by Rafael Palacios
Printed in the United States of America
10 9 8 7 6 5 4 3 2 1

Library of Congress Cataloging in Publication Data

Baker, Betty. Settlers and strangers. Includes index. Summary: A history of the Indians who have lived in the American Southwest from the Ice Age to the present day, told from their point of view.

1. Indians of North America—Southwest, New—History—Juvenile literature. [1. Indians of North America—Southwest, New—History] I. Title.
E78.S7B193 979'.004'97 77-4925 ISBN 0-02-708220-2

Contents

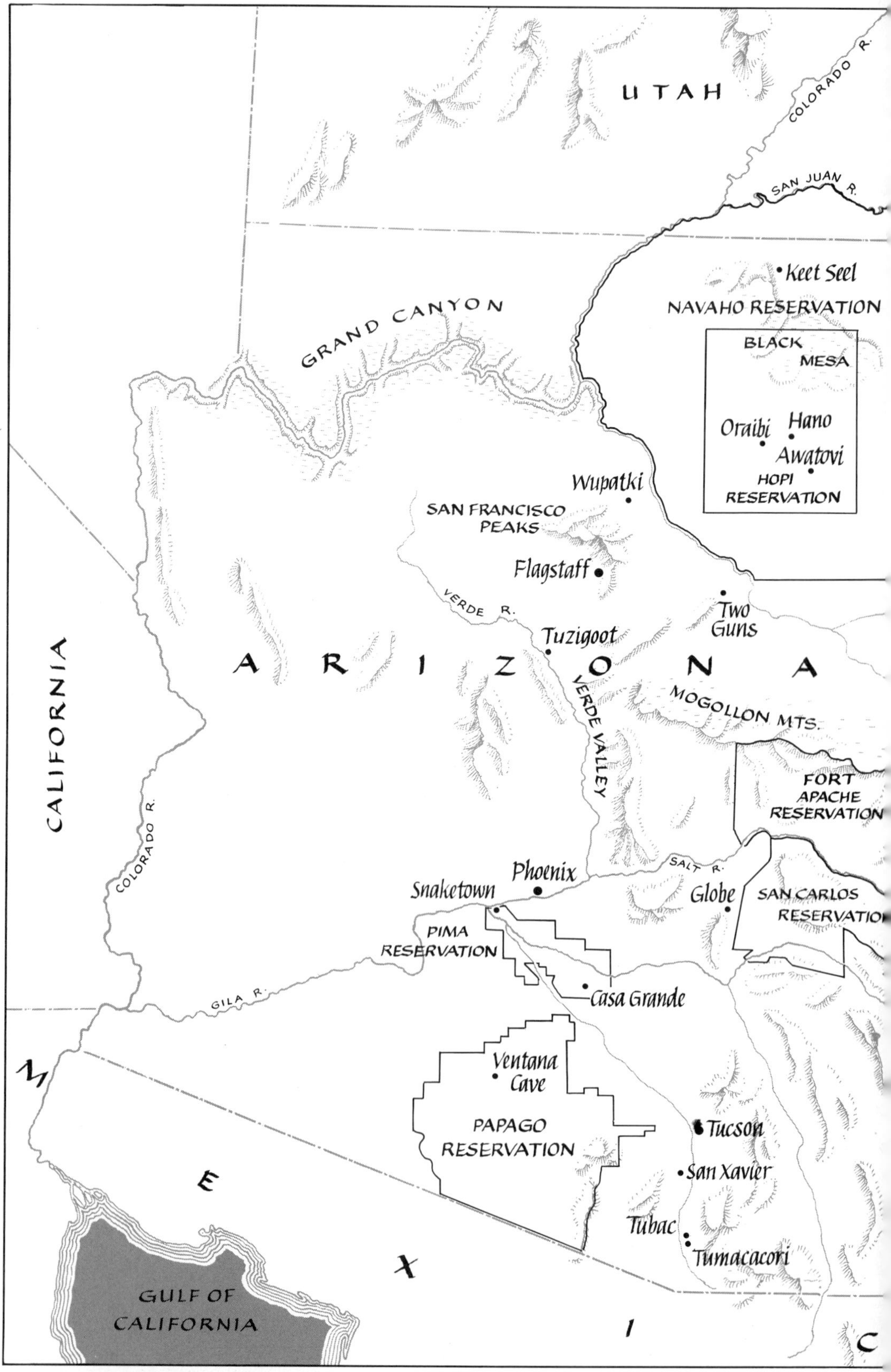

UTAH
COLORADO R.
SAN JUAN R.
Keet Seel
NAVAHO RESERVATION
BLACK MESA
Oraibi
Hano
Awatovi
HOPI RESERVATION
GRAND CANYON
Wupatki
SAN FRANCISCO PEAKS
Flagstaff
VERDE R.
Two Guns
Tuzigoot
CALIFORNIA
A R I Z O N A
VERDE VALLEY
MOGOLLON MTS.
FORT APACHE RESERVATION
COLORADO R.
SALT R.
Phoenix
Snaketown
Globe
SAN CARLOS RESERVATIO
PIMA RESERVATION
GILA R.
Casa Grande
Ventana Cave
PAPAGO RESERVATION
Tucson
San Xavier
Tubac
Tumacacori
M
E
X
I
C
GULF OF CALIFORNIA

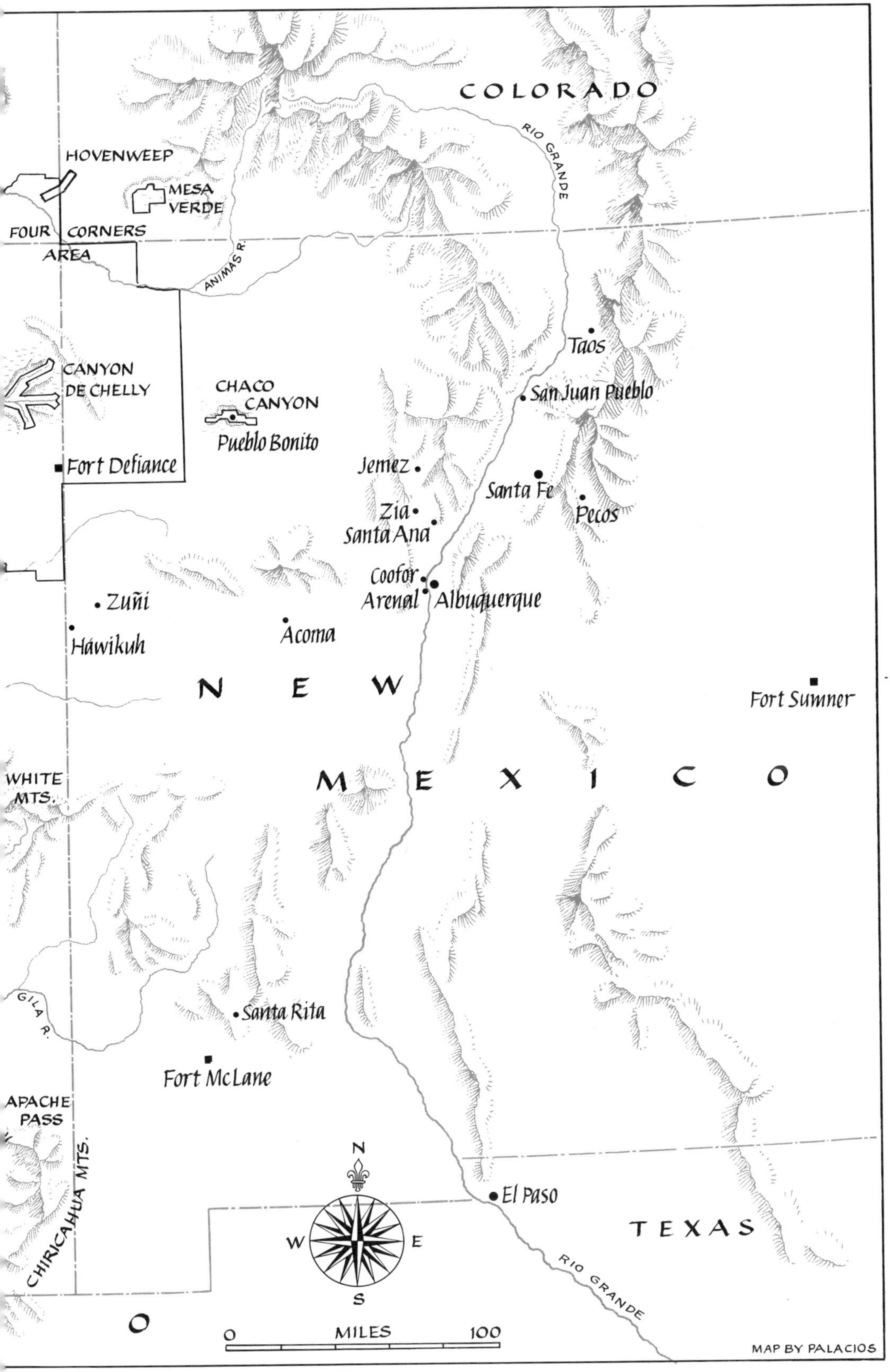

COLORADO
RIO GRANDE
HOVENWEEP
MESA VERDE
FOUR CORNERS AREA
ANIMAS R.
CANYON DE CHELLY
CHACO CANYON
Pueblo Bonito
Fort Defiance
Taos
San Juan Pueblo
Jemez
Santa Fe
Pecos
Zia
Santa Ana
Coofor
Arenal
Albuquerque
Zuñi
Hawikuh
Acoma
NEW MEXICO
Fort Sumner
WHITE MTS.
GILA R.
Santa Rita
Fort McLane
APACHE PASS
CHIRICAHUA MTS.
N
W
E
S
El Paso
TEXAS
RIO GRANDE
O
0 MILES 100
MAP BY PALACIOS

Warning

Most of what you find in history books is not in this one. This is not a history of the United States. It is the story of some tribes of native Americans who live in the desert southwest, mostly in Arizona and New Mexico. Only things that were important to them are told, and I have tried to tell them the way native Americans saw them.

Even today native Americans of the desert southwest make a difference between Spaniard, Mexican and white man. "Yankee" comes closer than "white man" to what is meant, so Yankee is what I have used. I have also used Yankee spellings.

We do not know what the first Americans called Canada or Arizona. We know what some of the later ones called certain places, but sometimes several tribes named a place and then the Spaniards renamed it and Yankees changed it again. The place is the same no matter what it is called, so I have used modern names, the ones found in modern books and maps.

Some tribes spread over the borders of Arizona and New Mexico but their religions and lives were influenced by other areas; they are not included here. This is the story of those tribes whose lives and religion were shaped by the southwestern desert and each other.

Betty Baker

ONE

Under and Over the Ground

People came into this world from underground. They climbed a ladder into the sunlight and wandered across the land. East, south, west and north they traveled. Then they built their pueblos, their towns, in northern Arizona and along the rivers of New Mexico. Stories of where people came up and what they did on their travels differ but the pueblos agree that people came into this world from underground.

Scientists do not. They say that before Columbus, people walked to America. They do not agree on when the first ones came. Some say thirty-six thousand years ago, others say seventy thousand years ago. But they all agree that people walked from Asia.

Seventy thousand years ago, say the scientists, the world was very cold. For hundreds of years water was drawn from the oceans into the air, then dropped as snow and sleet that did not melt and return to the oceans. It piled into glaciers, huge masses of ice. And as water was taken from the oceans and not replaced, the oceans lowered, leaving new pieces of land.

One of the new pieces of land joined Siberia to northwestern Alaska. Over the years, grasses covered the land. In summer birds and grass eaters moved onto the land and hunters followed.

People in Siberia were hunters. They needed meat for food, skins for clothes and houses, bones for tools and beads. They followed the caribou from summer to winter pasture and back again. Spring and fall, women took down the hide huts and packed them on sledges for the dogs to drag. If game was scarce, they had to move oftener to find new herds, but when grass was plentiful, the caribou herds used the same pastures year after year. Then the herds grew large and needed new land. So did the people.

There were enough hunters in a band of thirty to forty people to kill the largest game but when a band grew to fifty or sixty people, hunters had a hard time feeding everybody. Then the band divided, one group moving to a new hunting ground. Many of these bands moved onto the new land between Siberia and Alaska.

Grass grew thick. Hunting was good. The bands grew and divided again. Other bands from Siberia moved in behind them, pushing them on. And always there was the wonder of what was over the next rise, around the next curve of glacier.

Thirty-six thousand years ago most of Canada was covered by two glaciers, but between them was an ice-free strip of land. It led from eastern Alaska to the Dakotas. Down this passage came caribou, horses, timber wolves and foxes to join the animals already in America.

Slowly people moved their hide huts south between the mile-high walls of ice. In some places the glaciers were only twenty-five miles apart. The sun rose late and set early and always the air was dank and cold. Coming from between the glaciers onto the plains must have been like stepping from underground into a world of sun and sky. East, south and west, hunters spread over the United States.

For almost four thousand years the way south was open. Then the world grew warmer. Glaciers began to melt. Oceans grew. Slowly, so slowly a person would not notice in a life of thirty to forty years, water covered the land bridge from Siberia.

But in a few thousand years glaciers again began to grow. Oceans lowered. Once again people wandered south from Siberia to Alaska, then along the narrow Pacific coast or between the glaciers to the plains.

Still the glaciers grew. The land from Siberia to Alaska was larger than ever, but glaciers covered all Canada, the Great Lakes and part of the northern and western United States. For seven thousand years, until the glaciers melted for the last time, there was no way south from Alaska.

But people were already in the southwest. Winds from the glaciers kept the air chill and brought moisture. Rivers ran full. Grasses were thick and waist high. There was enough food and water for mouse and rabbit, horse, camel, quail and ground squirrel, deer and antelope, tapir, peccary, mammoth, bison and ground sloth. These and other animals fed the hunters: the wolf and eagle, jaguar, owl, coyote and man.

People changed things to fit the new land. New legends were made from their travels. Old gods were given homes on new mountains. Clothing changed to fit the warmer weather.

People built the same pit houses they had used in Siberia and on the way south, but digging was easier and faster in unfrozen ground. They dug a hole two feet deep and at

Prehistoric pictographs on sand rocks near Adamana, Arizona

least six feet across. Over this they built a dome-shaped frame of poles or mammoth bones. In Siberia and Alaska trees were scarce. There the frame had been covered with hides and the frame as well as the covering had been moved to each new camp. But the new land had more trees and bushes. The frame didn't have to be moved and it could be covered with branches and a thick layer of dirt added in cold weather. Precious hides could be saved for clothes or storage pouches.

Women had always gathered eggs, seeds and berries. Now they added sunflower seeds, pine nuts and yucca to their stores. These helped in the hungry times between kills.

There was plenty of meat after a large kill, but there was no way to save it. Although there were more kinds of game than in the far north, nobody had meat every day.

Small animals could be snared but the larger ones were fast and hard to hit. A man had to creep close enough to throw his spear without missing. Too often the animal discovered him and fled.

The huge ground sloth was slow-moving. A few hunters could keep it confused, darting in and out, stabbing with spears until it died. A large band could feast on the carcass for several days. Bison and mammoth were harder to bring down, even with a spear thrower.

Ten thousand years ago the spear thrower was America's most powerful weapon. Everyone knew some men threw spears farther and harder than other hunters. One man must have noticed that height and weight didn't always make the difference. What mattered was the length of the arm. Then he found a way to make every man's throwing arm almost two feet longer. He invented the spear thrower.

It was a stick or bone one to two feet long with a hook on one end. The spear was laid along it, the butt resting on the hook. The hunter held the other end, steadying the spear shaft with his thumb and finger. When he threw, the extra length of the thrower gave the swing a wider arc, adding speed, force and distance. The spear had a better chance of piercing the tough hide of mammoth or bison. But hunting was still not safe or easy.

It was safer to chase mammoth and bison into a marsh or over a cliff. Trapped in boggy ground or crippled by a fall, large animals could be easily killed by a few hunters.

Animals were chased by letting the wind carry the hunters' scent, by shouting and waving hides or by setting fire to the grass. This couldn't be done every day. There weren't many suitable marshes or cliffs and the game had to be in the right place. But when cliff or marsh, game and

A mammoth hunt as it might have happened 10,000 years ago, shown in a diorama

wind were right, hunters would gather the band to wave and shout or they would set fire to the grass.

Animals fled in panic. Not just mammoth or bison but all animals in the path of a fire went over the cliff. Bodies piled so high that the last animals could jump safely down and away. Far more animals died in each chase than any dozen bands could eat.

The mammoth probably took five years or more to bear young. It could not reproduce itself as fast as hunters killed it. The same was probably true of the ground sloth, big as an elephant and too slow to escape people and fire. Both vanished.

Horse, camel, antelope and longhorn bison reproduced faster. With enough food and water they might have survived the hunters. But herds in the southwest had never been large and the southwest was changing.

TWO

A New Way

For hundreds and thousands of years the glaciers melted. When the glaciers were gone, winds brought less moisture to the southwest and most of that was caught by mountains on their peaks or their north and west slopes. Less and less rain reached the southwest.

Streams died. Rivers shrank. Some ran only after heavy summer rain or when snow melted in the mountains. There were fewer trees and bushes and much less grass. Without food, many animals died. And as the land became desert, many kinds vanished.

Scientists say changes in the land and wasteful hunting killed off the animals. When ground sloth, mammoth, camel, horse and longhorn bison were gone, the huge dire wolf that fed on them disappeared, too. But rabbit, deer, peccary and other much-hunted animals still live in the desert. And jaguar, antelope, tapir and shorthorn bison live on in other places. Scientists agree there must be other reasons why some animals vanished, reasons they do not know.

Native Americans of the desert southwest say animals

must be treated with respect. They must be hunted with proper ceremony, and if they are wasted, killed without need, or their spirits insulted, they may vanish. It is a lesson learned six thousand years ago.

When the land changed and large animals were gone, hunting became even more uncertain. Deer and mountain sheep were fewer and harder to find. Hunting dances and ceremonies became important and so did the men who led them.

Instead of mammoth hunts, men joined in great hunts for rabbit. They wove yucca fiber and hemp into nets several hundred feet long. When staked across the end of a canyon or in a large half circle, the net made a fence three or four feet high. The hunters spread out. Then they yelled and beat at the bushes and grass, chasing rabbits and other small game into the net where they were caught and killed.

Peccary, a piglike animal, was too large for the nets but small and quick enough to be hard to hit with a spear. Slip nooses trapped mice and ground squirrels. Gophers, badgers and lizards were also eaten, but it took many small animals to feed twenty to thirty people twice or even once a day. The search for food never ended.

Women gathering food, shown in a diorama

Life among the Basketmakers of the Mesa Verde, Colorado, region, 2,000 years ago, shown in a diorama

Each band settled into a hunting territory and moved around it with the seasons. In the mountains women gathered pine nuts and juniper berries. In the low desert they roasted yucca stems and picked cactus fruit. But mostly they filled their baskets with sunflower, millet and other seeds, some as fine as sand.

Seeds were ground between stones to make a coarse flour. This was made into flat cakes and baked in ashes or added to a basket of boiling water to make a soup like thin cooked cereal.

Women made baskets for all uses, from small serving trays to large, squat storage baskets with lids. Bunches of twigs or reeds were coiled to the proper size and shape. Each row of coil was covered with loops of yucca, cattail leaf or willow strips that stitched it to the coil beneath. Some women stitched so finely and tightly that their baskets were waterproof, but most baskets used for cooking or water storage were coated with the gum of piñon pine, the same tree that gave nuts.

Basket cooking was slow and tiresome. Stones were heated in a bed of coals. Using sticks, the cook lifted the hot stones and dropped them in a basket of water. Cooled stones were taken out, reheated and dropped in again, over and over until the water boiled and the soup cooked.

When game became scarce or the season changed, the band moved to the next campsite. Before leaving, women buried their grinding stones and best heating stones. If the harvest had been very good, baskets of seeds were buried in stone-lined pits. They could be found when needed and nobody would have to carry them. But most seasons there wasn't enough left to store.

When they reached the next campsite, house pits were cleaned out and the tops rebuilt. Women dug up their grinding stones or found new ones. Men checked their nets and worked their ceremonies to bring food to their spears and traps.

In their planned wanderings, bands often met. Sometimes hunters met by chance. Sometimes related bands joined to hold special ceremonies, play games and find husbands and wives. But any meeting was a time for trading. Everything was traded: feathers, beads, rabbit-skin blankets, bone dice, songs and ceremonies and, most important, news and ideas.

On both sides of the southern Arizona–New Mexico border lived a group of bands called the Cochise people. In their travels up and down the mountains and canyons, they met people from the south. These people traded with people from farther south, people who had a seed, a special seed, that they had gotten from people still farther south.

A man could plant a few of these seeds and, with the proper songs and care, grow a basket of seed. Best of all,

Pit houses in Mesa Verde, Colorado, about 600 A.D., *shown in a diorama*

the seeds could be grown just outside the door of the pit house. No more hunger, no more days of tracking game!

The Cochise people must have talked of nothing else the next few seasons and they must have scraped together every bit of trade goods they could find or make. The songs and ceremonies for growing would cost as much as the seed itself. But when the people to the south had seed to trade, the Cochise people were ready. About five thousand years ago, they began growing corn along the streams in their canyons.

But farming was not an easy life. The first corn traded north from Mexico grew ears shorter than a man's finger. And the ears were not covered by husks. Once they formed, women and children had to spend their days chasing birds from the fields. Men still had to hunt because corn didn't give people all the food they needed,

Early farmers at work, shown in a diorama

and at night they had to camp in the fields and chase desert animals from the sweet green plants.

In the growing season, corn made more work, not less. But there was almost always food to store, not just seed for the next crop but corn for eating. And over the tens and hundreds of years, better seed came from the south, seed that grew larger ears, ears covered by husks and protected from birds. But still the fields had to be guarded and men still had to spend most of their days hunting. And always game seemed scarcer.

Then, a thousand years after corn, seeds of two other plants came from Mexico. The Cochise people began growing squash and beans with their corn. These three foods, raised in the desert, changed the way people lived and thought and sang, and made the farmers of the desert southwest different from any other native Americans.

THREE

The People from Underground

Beans eaten with corn and squash gave people all the protein they had been getting from meat. Without beans the men would have stayed hunters and part-time farmers. But corn was the food they honored, the plant they worried about and sang for.

Corn was their wheat and potatoes. They ate it at every meal in a dozen different ways, from roasted ears to a drink of fine flour mixed with water. Fine flour took three grindings. At each grinding the stone wore away, adding bits of stone to the corn.

It gave them a new saying, "Every man must eat a grinding stone in his lifetime." But the eating, over a lifetime, wore away the enamel on teeth. Old people of forty or forty-five were more certain of having toothache than rheumatism or arthritis. It was a small price to pay for life, and corn was life.

Men and boys still hunted rabbits and other small animals for food but large game was hunted only when there was time. Hides and horns of deer and buffalo were needed for ceremonies and hooves for rattles, so the hunting chants and dances were not forgotten. But they were not often used. Hunting was no longer as important as farming. Instead of searching the ground for game sign, men watched for clouds above the mountains.

Fields were planted on low land beside a stream. When melted snow filled the stream, the fields were flooded and seeds could be planted. Heavy summer rain drained off the rocky mountain slopes into the streams and sometimes reached the fields. But rain fell seldom in the mountains and less often on the fields. Ceremonies were needed to call rain. The stars were watched for the proper time to hold them.

There were ceremonies for planting and growing, to call rain and to show respect to sun and earth and the spirits of corn and rain. The ceremonies did not need to be short. The fields would not run away. There was time to try new songs, add dances traded from the south and work for many days to get them perfect.

Since people no longer moved, there was no worry about making things that could not be carried. Headdresses and costumes could be made for every dance. Special pit houses were built to store them. Men practiced in these houses, prayed and were purified in them, and some of the ceremonies were held there.

As dances and chants were added, the ceremonies grew longer. Some lasted ten or twenty days, with even more time needed to prepare them. When every word and step was perfect, the spirits were pleased. The corn grew and the storerooms were full.

With plenty of food, the Cochise people increased. New villages were built up and down the streams. But finding the right kind of farmland was harder than moving to a new hunting area. New villages were built farther and farther away. Slowly the Cochise people spread north and went into the Mogollon Mountains bordering central Arizona and New Mexico.

Two thousand years after the Cochise people became farmers, the white man's calendar changed from B.C. to A.D. and the Cochise people learned about pottery. Like farming, news of pottery making came from Mexico, and it too changed the people's food.

Pots could be set on the fire. Without the work of heating stones, water could be boiled easily and for as long as needed. Meat could be stewed. Beans were always cooked soft. Women could make corn stew and corn dumplings.

Water jars were better than pitch-lined baskets. Water seeped through the unglazed sides and dried in the desert breeze, cooling the water in the jar.

But pottery broke. Some broke while being made.

Women shaped the pots much like baskets, coiling clay into shape and pinching the coils together. Some left their cooking pots like this but most smoothed the clay carefully, inside and out. The pots were then set to dry in the sun, away from playing children, dogs and careless feet.

When dry, the pots were painted with the juice of plants or with ground minerals mixed with plant juices. Brushes, some small enough to draw fine lines and cross-hatching, were made by chewing the end of a twig or bit of yucca leaf.

When enough pots were ready, a bed of coals was prepared. The pots were stacked on rocks to keep them from touching the hot coals, then covered with slabs of stone or pieces of old broken pots so smoke would not blacken their sides. Then the whole mound was covered with firewood and set on fire. The flames died; the coals and pots cooled. The woman dug carefully.

The pots came out brownish, reddish, gray, white or

Early pottery made by the Anasazi (first two rows) and the Mimbres (bottom row)

black, depending on what kind of clay was used and how much air reached them during the firing. Since neighbors used the same kind of clay and traded ideas, they usually made the same sort of pottery. In a few hundred years, the Mimbres, a group of Cochise people living in the Mogollon Mountains, were making some of the most beautiful pottery ever found. They painted black animals and birds and designs with fine borders on the inside of shallow white bowls.

But even fine pots were heavy. Baskets were better for gathering food or carrying it to and from the grinding stones or for use in dances and most ceremonies. Cochise and Mogollon women didn't stop making baskets; they just made fewer kinds.

Someone invented the bow and arrow. The idea spread, changing slightly as each people found the best wood and size and shape for themselves. The bow was better for hunting small animals, and Cochise and Mogollon men stopped making spears.

People began farming in the Four Corners area, the few hundred miles of mesas and canyons around the place where New Mexico, Colorado, Utah and Arizona meet. These people were probably not Cochise but hunting bands who learned farming and pottery by trading with the Cochise.

The Four Corners people built pit houses, too. Often they built them on ledges in the canyon wall. This took people out of the dark canyon floor into the sunshine and warmth. It also gave them a good view up and down the canyon. Strange people sometimes wandered down from the north and they weren't always friendly. It was good to be able to see who was coming.

In time, pits for houses were dug shallower and finally

not at all. Instead of wood frames, stones were piled into walls and plastered over. Someone, perhaps a bride who didn't like house building, decided to save the work of building one wall and built her house onto her mother's. Soon everyone was building attached houses.

Often the houses were built in a U or square around a plaza which was the living center of the pueblo, the town of attached houses. Here people worked, talked, traded and held dances. The U or square also made a small fort that was easy to defend, especially if house doors were put in the roof. Ladders used to reach the roof could be pulled up and the pueblo defended from strange people who wanted the corn, beans and dried squash that filled the storerooms.

The richer the pueblos became, the greater was the

The building of a one-story pueblo in Mesa Verde, Colorado, about 850 A.D., shown in a diorama; in front are two underground kivas.

Spruce Tree House, built in a cave in Mesa Verde, Colorado, as it looked 700 years ago, shown in a diorama

danger of attack. So when the pueblos grew, houses were added on top instead of alongside. Rooms on the ground were used for storage or filled in with dirt and stones. The upper houses had doors in the walls opening onto the roofs of those below. This gave outside living space and much pueblo work and visiting was done here.

People had everything they needed and everything they had came from the earth: their safe houses, rabbit-fur blankets, twine for bags, sandals and women's string skirts, baskets and pots and the food to put in them, bows and arrows, hoes and digging sticks. Even charms and medicines came from the earth. The pueblo people began to think of the earth as their mother and the pit houses used for ceremonies were dug deeper. They became kivas, underground ceremonial rooms.

Each dance or ceremony was owned by a society, a

group of men who were members by birth or through passing certain tests. Every man belonged to at least one society and certain societies seemed to produce most of the town leaders.

When a man married he went to live in his wife's house. If she was from a different pueblo, the man found a welcome in his society's kiva. If his wife's pueblo did not have his society, he might begin one. When there were enough members, the society would build a kiva and add its dance or ceremony to those already held. Or a ceremony might be bought from another people or pueblo and a society begun for it.

A kiva was a place for men to meet and talk, to sleep if their wives' houses were too crowded, if they'd had a fight or if they were preparing for a ceremony. A kiva was cool in summer, warm in winter and always private. It was the place to set up a loom for weaving, to settle the business of the pueblo or to plan hunting and trading trips. But most important, a kiva was the place for ceremonies.

Dances were practiced in the kivas. Men taking part in the ceremonies prayed, fasted and were purified in the kivas. This was the private part of the ceremony when only members were allowed in the kiva. Any others who came near were beaten by guards.

If the public part of the ceremony was held in the kiva, people were invited to watch. It was one of the few times women were allowed inside. But often the ceremony ended with a dance in the plaza. Then the pueblo had a holiday. But even with the laughter and the clowning of certain dancers, the ceremony was serious.

Chants and dances were prayers. If they were not done exactly right or if a dancer, singer or drummer had not lived the right way, the prayer would not be answered.

Rain would not fall or evil would come to the pueblo.

For a few hundred years everything went right. By 1100 there were large pueblos in canyons all around Four Corners, across northern Arizona and south into Cochise country in New Mexico. The greatest and one of the first was Pueblo Bonito on the floor of Chaco Canyon in northern New Mexico. This four-level D-shaped pueblo grew to eight hundred rooms and thirty-two kivas. People traveled many miles for the ceremonies at Pueblo Bonito and even farther for the trading, piling their goods on mats outside the pueblo walls or in the crowded plazas.

Anything could be found in a place the size of Pueblo

The ruins of Pueblo Bonito in Chaco Canyon, New Mexico; the round holes were kivas.

Bonito: tobacco, turkey-feather cloaks, mountain sheep and bear skins, raw cotton and cotton blankets painted with fine black designs, white pottery with the same kind of black designs, rabbit-fur blankets, bright bird feathers, beads of shell, bone or colored stone, loose or inlaid in pendants. Most precious of all were live parrots from Mexico. Their feathers were needed for ceremonies and men mined turquoise to trade for the birds or their feathers. Almost as valuable were copper bells from Mexico and salt and shells from the Gulf of California.

Even if a man had nothing to trade, there was always news to gather. Everything that happened was talked over in Pueblo Bonito: in a small pueblo in Canyon de Chelly, most of the children had died. But the witch who sent the sickness had been found and killed. . . . The people of Mesa Verde were having trouble with Utes. They were always being raided. That's why they built their red stone pueblos in high caves. . . . A medicine man in Tuzigoot had a cure for stomach pains and another at Keet Seel knocked out rotten teeth so fast it hardly hurt. . . . Two pairs of twins had been born at Hovenweep, a lucky sign. . . . But people were leaving Wupatki and other pueblos in the black land. Old men could remember when everyone was talking of moving there.

During the winter of 1064, a volcano had erupted in northern Arizona. The Sinagua, settlers from the Mogollon people, had been driven from their pit houses. When they returned, the land was covered with cinders like coarse black sand. Instead of ruining the land for farming, the cinders held moisture and made farming even better.

The news spread and people began moving onto the black land—not just the Sinagua who'd left, but pueblo people looking for better land and some of the people from

The ruins of Wupatki, Arizona; in the center is the rebuilt "amphitheater" where ceremonies were held.

Mexico who had settled in southern Arizona. They spread over eight hundred square miles, planted their fields and built small pueblos: Wupatki, Wukoki, Turkey Hill and hundreds of others. They raised their children in the right way, but when their grandchildren were learning the ceremonies, something went wrong.

There was less rain than usual but just as much wind. Sand and cinders blew around, leaving some land bare and piling cinder drifts in other places. Bare fields didn't hold enough moisture for farming and drifted fields couldn't be dug. Every season more families packed up and left.

Some left in groups and built new pueblos in canyons to the south. Others went to pueblos where their mothers' clans would take them in. And in the plazas and on the rooftops, people talked about it.

Surely the volcano had been the work of spirits underground. The good farming afterward proved it. But those

Hohokam, those people from Mexico, must have angered the spirits. Instead of foot races to help the sun, they had built a fancy plaza for ball games. And pueblo people, who should have known better, had gone to Wupatki to watch the games. All around Four Corners, men talked in the kivas and decided the spirits had been right to take away the good black sand.

They also talked about the empty houses at Pueblo Bonito. People were leaving Chaco Canyon, too. Some were already building a new pueblo on the Animas River to the north. If they were wise, they would not build too big. Too much building had caused their trouble in Chaco Canyon.

Pueblo Bonito was only the largest pueblo in Chaco Canyon. There were dozens of others, and all needed wood for ceiling beams. In just fifty years, thousands and thousands of trees were cut from the walls of a canyon only eight miles long and two miles wide. Without tree roots to hold the earth, the rains that flooded the river and watered the fields also washed away soil and cut deep gulleys down the canyon sides.

The rushing water brought rocks and soil that scoured the bottom of the river. Slowly, over the years, the river cut itself a channel. As the riverbed lowered, so did the surface of the water. The river no longer flooded the farthest fields. Then came the seasons with little rain, the ones that dried the black sand.

Twenty-four years the drought lasted. Everybody in the desert southwest had trouble, but the people in Chaco Canyon had more than most. When rain did fall, the dry cracked earth, stripped of its trees, washed away faster than before. The river cut deeper and more farmers lost their fields.

Because of the drought, game was scarce. Bands of Utes, hunters from the north, raided the Four Corners area. The people were safe in their cliff pueblos, but what good was safety if the harvest could not be brought in? Or if it was stolen from the fields? And with so little rain, there was less to harvest.

Slowly the people began moving south. Then, when there were no longer enough men to hold the ceremonies, the rest followed. By 1300 most of the Four Corners pueblos were empty. Soon after, all the people had moved.

Some built pueblos along the Rio Grande, all the way to Texas. Others joined pueblos around the springs at Black Mesa or built in the mountains and mesas of northern Arizona. People still live in some of these pueblos.

Each pueblo, from Acoma to Zuñi, is a little different. Some are one level high, some two or three. The people weave different designs, paint their pottery differently, hold some different ceremonies and even speak different languages. But important things are the same.

Pueblo men are farmers and most ceremonies have something to do with growing corn. Every pueblo has at least one kiva and each kiva has a small opening in the floor, a symbol of how people came into the world.

FOUR

Strangers

Hundreds of pueblos were built in the canyons of northern Arizona, New Mexico and along the Rio Grande. The moving, mixing and resettling stirred new ideas. Pottery, weaving and jewelry took on new designs. Ceremonies grew larger, the costumes more elaborate and kachinas appeared in the plazas.

Kachinas are spirits, messengers between the gods and the people. Hopi kachinas live in the San Francisco peaks east of the Hopi pueblos. Kachinas of other pueblos, such as the Zuñi, live in lakes or underground.

Long ago, kachinas left their homes to spend half the year with the people, guiding them and bringing good fortune and rain. But when the kachinas returned to their homes, people followed them to the land of the spirits. Every year more people followed them and that was wrong. Living people should not go to the land of the spirits.

The kachinas said they would no longer visit the pueblos. Instead, certain good men would carve masks to look like kachinas and take their places in ceremonies and

This exhibit shows small kachina figures in front of a photograph of a Hopi plaza, where kachina dances take place in warm weather. The kachinas dance on each side of the plaza in turn. The dance is repeated again and again until dusk, when the dancers return to the kiva.

dances. Each man must guard and feed his mask, for the spirit of the kachina would be in it. And when the man died, the mask must be buried so its spirit could return to the kachina. This way kachinas could help the people without being a danger to them. And so it is.

No one knows how many kachinas there are. More than two hundred have been counted in Hopi and Zuñi pueblos where kachinas are best known. But new ones appear and others vanish.

There is a kachina with a head like a mud ball. Another is painted with black and white stripes and its hair is pulled into a topknot. Some are strange and beautiful and others are fearsome.

Every year the kachinas come. Some bring bean plants, green with leaves, when snow is still on the ground.

Carved kachinas are often given as gifts to children. Shown here are: (top left) Eagle; (top right) Hemis; (bottom, left to right) Mudhead, Cow, Deer, Corn Dancer and Tsu-ku (Rio Grande clown).

Others bring gifts for children. Some punish, some cause laughter. Others mock those who deserve to look foolish. In an important Zuñi ceremony, giant kachinas race. But always the kachinas are greeted with joy and there is sorrow at their leaving.

With ceremonies for kachinas, farming, hunting and healing, there was hardly a week in the pueblos without a dance or sing. Stars and sun marked the times for planting and ceremony and the years passed, each a little different yet much the same.

Not everything was right. A pueblo on the east bank of the Rio Grande kept a large snake that brought it good fortune. One night the snake left and went downriver and the people had to leave the pueblo. Always there were witches causing sickness. Some pueblos killed so many witches the people who were left had to move. But for over a hundred years most pueblos prospered. Then people again began to move.

This was not a search for new land like the southward movement during the long drought. This was a gathering together for protection. By 1400, instead of hundreds of pueblos scattered over thousands of miles, there were about seventy. Most were in three groups: the Hopi in northeastern Arizona, the Zuñi on the Arizona–New Mexico border, and the string of pueblos on both sides of the Rio Grande, from Taos to Texas.

No one knows why hundreds of pueblos were deserted in such a short time, but it is known that strangers were settling in the desert southwest.

These strangers had once been one people but, in their wanderings, had become two. Both tribes called themselves The People. Their new neighbors called them *Navaho,* Takers from the Fields, and *Apache,* Enemy.

Canyon de Chelly in northern Arizona

They came to the southwest in small bands over many years. They were wanderers from northwest Canada. Overcrowding must have forced them to look for new land. For tens and hundreds of years they must have been moving south, pushed on by hunger or by stronger neighbors who did not like their ways.

The pueblos met the Navahos with friendship and taught them to farm. But the strangers had come too late. The best land was already taken. When hunting and their bit of poor farming weren't enough to feed them, they raided their neighbors.

There was more than food behind pueblo walls. The Navahos carried off cotton blankets, turquoise beads, women and children. The captives brought with them pueblo ways.

Pueblo people do not believe in fighting. It is not the right way to live. But every pueblo had a war leader and if attacked, they would fight. When raiding Navahos were caught, they were killed or taken captive. Some of these escaped and told what they had seen and heard in the pueblos.

Sometimes there was trade, though never inside the pueblo walls. From trade and the captives, Navahos learned bits and pieces of pueblo ways, myths and ceremonies. These were woven into their own and, shaped by the new land, grew into something new and Navaho.

The Navahos were still hunters and raiders. They wandered the Four Corners area and northern New Mexico and Arizona, a land of red rock and sand cut by canyons where there were water, trees and the empty pueblos of "the ancient ones."

Because they moved with the game and the season, the pueblo ceremony of sand painting suited the Navahos best. Materials to make the dry paintings were easily collected in their wanderings, and small bags of corn meal, pollen, dried flowers, crushed red and yellow sandstone, charcoal and minerals were easy to carry. The paintings were drawn on buckskin or a layer of fine light sand. Neither was hard to find.

Sand paintings became powerful Navaho ceremonies. They are used for many things, but mostly for healing. The man who knows the painting, its songs and ceremony, dribbles finely ground plants and minerals between thumb and finger. Many colors outline the design and fill in the spaces. The design must be perfect or it will have no power.

There are over five hundred designs for Navaho sand paintings, ranging in size from one foot across to over twenty. One man will know only a few, and for large ones he will have helpers. A sand painting must be drawn, used and destroyed before sunset.

The Navahos have made sand paintings and healing ceremonies so much their own that a pueblo once hired a group of Navahos to cure disease. But pueblo men watched and listened closely to learn the ceremony so they would not need to ask the enemy inside the walls again.

A Navaho sand painting called "Whirling Logs" (1968)

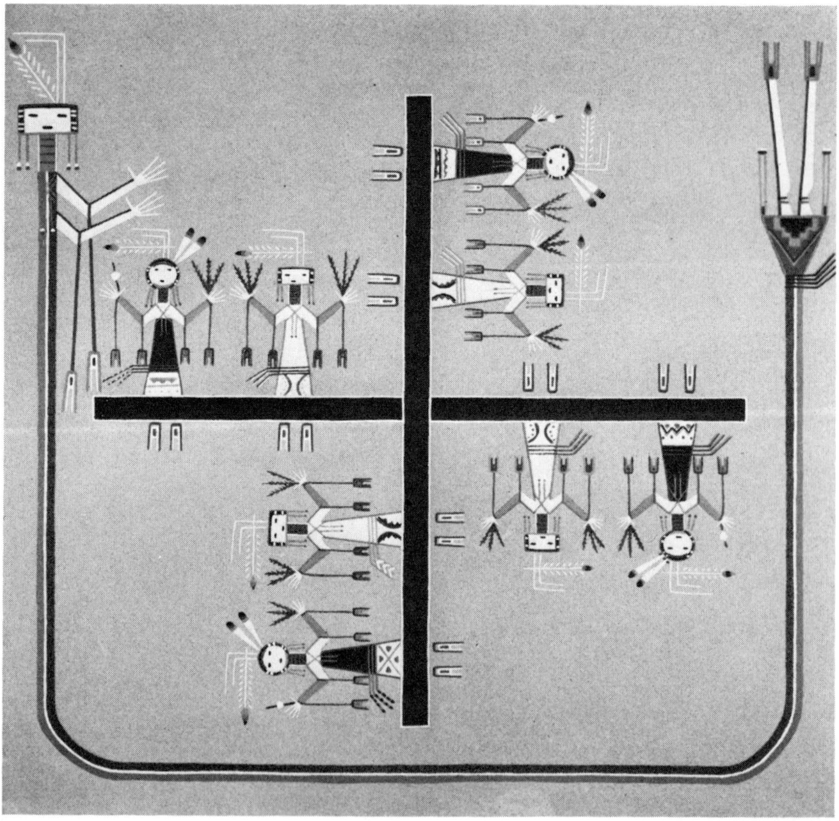

Just as sand painting became Navaho, Navaho weaving later became more famous than the pueblo weaving from which it was learned. But among the Navahos, it is the women, not the men, who are the weavers.

An old Apache story says, "Long ago there was a woman who cooked little children for her son and herself to eat. The Apaches drove the woman and her son out of camp and it is from them that the Navahos come."

The story tells more about what Apaches think of Navahos than it does about how Navahos began. It probably means the Apaches did not approve of the Navahos taking up strange ways. Certainly the Apaches did not change much. Some bands borrowed sand paintings from either the pueblos or Navahos but the Apaches used only a few, and those not often.

Perhaps the Navahos arrived first and then forced the Apaches farther south into even harsher desert. For it is true the tribes were not friendly. Apaches often raided Navahos, especially for wives. And the Navahos raided back for revenge.

In the 1800s, Navahos caught an Apache raiding party in a cave near Two Guns, Arizona, and penned them in to die. (Forty years later a white man found the death cave and sold the Apache skulls to tourists on Route 66.)

Central and southern New Mexico and Arizona are three thousand feet lower than the northern parts and much hotter and dryer. It is a land of heat and cactus cut by a few mountains and rocky peaks. It is here most Apache bands learned to live.

Both Navahos and Apaches began with brush huts much like pit houses without pits. The Navahos made theirs larger and stronger until they became the hogans of today, large six- or eight-sided buildings like igloos built of

A Navaho hogan, corral and summer shelter in Canyon de Chelly, Arizona

logs and covered with dirt to hold out the cold of high desert winters.

The Apaches never changed their wickiups. The small brush houses let the desert breeze through in summer. In winter, the brush was covered with hides. Like Navahos, Apaches wore deerskin clothes, but Apache moccasins became knee-high to give better protection against cactus and rattlesnakes.

Apache boys were trained to survive alone in the desert, to travel fifty miles a day and carry pebbles in their mouths to hold back thirst.

Women gathered cactus fruit, nuts, berries and seeds and roasted the stem of the mescal or century plant. Men and boys hunted. Anything living was game, from deer and duck in the mountains to ground squirrels and lizards in the desert. All except fish. Like Navahos, Apaches would not eat fish. And when game was scarce, they raided the farmers.

In central and southern Arizona, the farmers were Pimas and Papagos and their villages had no walls.

FIVE

Eetoi's People

The Pima and Papago say, "Eetoi made us. He made us from the red earth."

But the long story, once told in ceremony songs, tells how the people Eetoi made turned against him. Four times they killed Eetoi and four times he came back. Then he went underground and found another people. He led these men up from underground and chased the first people away. North, west and south he chased them. Then the men from underground settled in southern Arizona.

They took wives from women the first people had left behind but they did not live in the way of those first people. They lived in the way Eetoi taught them and left the mud buildings of the first people to fall in the desert.

The Pima called these old towns *hohokam,* all used up. The name is now used for the people who built them, the people the Pima and Papago say were chased away by Eetoi. The old songs name the towns where Eetoi fought battles, towns along the Salt and Gila rivers, towns that no longer exist.

Scientists do not believe the old songs. If they are

history, say the scientists, they are so mixed with old songs and songs borrowed from other people that no one can know how much is true. But scientists do not know where the Pima and Papago came from. They can only guess, but the Pima and Papago may be the oldest people still living in the desert southwest.

People lived in Ventana Cave, south of Phoenix, Arizona, for ten thousand years. They were food gatherers and hunters of small game. They were living in Ventana Cave when the Hohokam began building their towns, and probably other bands were living nearby. Did they learn farming from the Hohokam and become the Pima and Papago? Or are the Pima and Papago descended from the Hohokam? Or did a new people come from the east and chase the Hohokam north, west and south and are the Pima and Papago descended from them? The Pima and Papago could be a mixture of the first two or of all three.

Animals near Ventana Cave, Arizona, 10,000 years ago, shown in a diorama

Whatever the truth, the Hohokam are part of Pima and Papago history.

In 300 B.C. the Hohokam were building their shallow pit houses along the Salt and Gila rivers. They might have been Cochise people who had wandered from the mountains or hunters who had learned farming from the Cochise people. But it is more likely they were settlers from Mexico.

Everything known about them shows a different way of thinking, a way so different that no other people in the desert southwest copied them. Yet the Hohokam lived in Arizona for over a thousand years.

Hohokam building a pit house

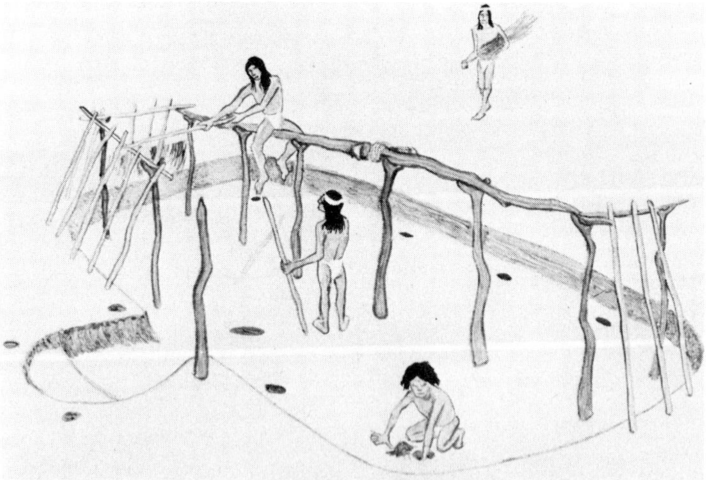

Their oldest and largest city was Snaketown, where the Gila and Salt rivers meet. For a thousand years, pit houses were built and deserted and built again. The city finally covered more than three hundred acres. Among the pit houses were pyramids like those in Mexico. Because they had no stone nearby, the Hohokam built the pyramids of earth, perhaps the same earth they dug to make the canals.

Some pueblo farmers piled up low walls of dirt to guide flood waters to fields but no other farmers in the desert southwest dug canals. It was an idea nobody wanted. Canals meant digging into the earth and the earth was their mother. It was one thing to dig a hole to plant a seed for mother earth to grow. It was a terrible thing to dig ditches and carry off mountains of dirt.

But the Hohokam dug canals, hundreds of miles of canals to water their fields. At Casa Grande, their town between Phoenix and Tucson, the main canal left the Gila River seventeen miles above the town, and dozens of smaller canals led off it. There were dozens of systems like this one. All of them were dug with sticks and the dirt was carried away in baskets.

Modern scientists uncover the abandoned canals at Snaketown, Arizona.

The Hohokam must have thought differently about the earth. Their songs and ceremonies must have been different. Like some people of ancient Mexico, they made clay figures for ceremonies, and they were the only people in the desert southwest to build ball courts.

The ball game was a ceremony of ancient Mexico. The court was shaped like two T's, stem to stem. Stone rings were set high in the walls at the center. Two teams tried to hit a ball through the rings, using only legs and hips. Though players wore padding, they often injured and sometimes killed each other. It was not the sort of game pueblo people would like or approve.

The Hohokam and pueblo people knew each other. There was much trading. The Hohokam used pottery from the northern pueblos and it was probably through the Hohokam that the pueblos got copper bells and parrots. The Hohokam also etched designs on shells for pendants. They were the first people in the world to etch.

During the land boom in the black sand country, Hohokam moved north and lived among the pueblo people. In the great drought that followed, pueblo people moved to the Salt and Gila rivers and settled among the Hohokam. Soon after this the Hohokam built a four-story building at Casa Grande.

The first story was filled with dirt. The fourth had openings in the walls to tell the time for planting and ceremonies. But a four-story building wasn't needed for that.

Were the pueblo people living with them homesick for high buildings? Perhaps they didn't feel safe without a lookout tower to give them a wide view of the land.

But the town was also walled. No one could leave or enter without using ladders. Were there enemies in the

The ruins of Casa Grande, Arizona, shown in a drawing made in 1878

land? It was about this time, 1350 to 1400, that pueblo people were leaving the Verde Valley and White Mountains just to the north. That later became Apache country. Were Apaches already attacking the Hohokam, driving them away? Or, like Pueblo Bonito, had Casa Grande created its own enemy?

After years of constant watering, desert earth becomes too alkaline to grow crops. It is a problem faced by modern ranchers. But the Hohokam had no chemicals to add to the earth. They could only dig their canals to reach new fields. Sooner or later they reached places too high for canals to be dug. It was move or starve.

Old men in pueblo kivas were not surprised. Hohokam farmers had changed things from the way they should be. If they had not dug into mother earth, she would still be growing their corn.

Moving was no longer easy. The great drought had sent thousands of people south. The best farmland was gone. And it may not have been safe along the Gila River. This was the time when pueblo people were gathering into three main groups. Those along the Gila were joining the Hopi, Zuñi and northern New Mexico pueblos.

No one knows where the Hohokam went, but by 1425 they were gone. Casa Grande and Snaketown were empty. A few may have gone north with their pueblo neighbors, especially if there had been marriages between the peoples.

There were Hohokam living along the Colorado River in 1200. Some families from the Gila River towns may have joined them. There were large Hohokam towns just south of the Arizona border. That is probably where most Arizona Hohokam went. Then all, including those along the Colorado River, moved south into Mexico.

North, west and south, just as the old Pima and Papago songs say. And just as the old songs also say, some Hohokam must have stayed behind and mixed with other people. But by 1500 the Hohokam towns were deserted and Pima and Papago were calling them "all used up."

Pima and Papago language, ceremonies and myths are much the same. The difference in name came from where they lived, which decided what they ate.

The Papagos were called Bean People because beans from mesquite trees were one of their important foods. They lived where streams ran dry part of the year. Farming was chancy, the crops small. They had to gather much of their food, moving with the seasons. In hungry winters they went to live and work with the Pima, the River People.

The Pima lived in villages along the Salt and Gila rivers. They raised corn, beans, squash, tobacco and the finest cotton in the southwest. Tobacco and cotton were traded to the pueblos in the north and to Papagos living south in Mexico. And with the trading went news.

(Top) An early Pima village in Arizona; (bottom) a modern Papago camp near Ventana Cave, Arizona, during the saguaro harvest

After 1519 the Papagos in Mexico had stories of strange men to the south, men with hair on their faces who rode on the backs of big animals and fought with sticks that spit fire. Over the seasons the stories became more frightening.

The strange men attacked the villages. Harvests and seed corn were carried away and the fields trampled by the horses. Men were killed or lamed. Women and children were taken slaves.

The strange men raided farther north every year but they still were far to the south, so far that not even the Papagos in Mexico worried. But in early spring, 1536, some of these strange men came not from the south but from the east.

SIX

The Enemy

There were four of them. They had no animals or lightning sticks. They wore loincloths and sandals like real people. One had black skin. Though some scraped and scratched at it, the color did not come off. Hair grew long and thick on their faces and two had pale eyes that made one think of ghosts. But they did not seem evil. Two were said to be great healers, and the black one, Esteban, knew many Papago ways and some of their language.

The strangers had been shipwrecked near Galveston, Texas, eight years before. Last year they'd escaped from the coast tribe that had found them. Since then they'd been traveling west from people to people, healing many on the way. They asked many questions about the pueblos.

The Papagos told them about the Zuñi, how huge and rich their six pueblos were. Some questions they did not understand but they answered "yes" because it made the strangers happy.

The strangers walked south, from village to village, and out of Papago country. Three years later Esteban returned.

He was going to visit the Zuñi and asked Papago men to guide him. A few days behind him was a priest. Would the Papago guide him, too?

It was the end of winter. Some men had cotton to trade. Others felt like visiting. It would be several months until their own rain ceremony was held but the Zuñi had many dances. And a dance meant a feast. Besides, they liked Esteban. By the time he reached Háwikuh, Esteban had more than a hundred Pima and Papago with him.

The Zuñi saw them coming. Leaders of important kivas met them outside the pueblo. They listened to Esteban and understood that he came from the strange men to the south. They knew about the Spaniards, their horses and their raids. They had decided to kill any who came to the Zuñi pueblos, but Esteban was black like some kachinas. He might be a holy person. But if he was, how could he come from the evil strangers to the south?

Two Zuñi grabbed Esteban under the arms, carried him into the pueblo and pulled up the ladders. They put him in a room under guard while they decided what he was.

All night, men talked in a kiva. They agreed a holy person could not be killed and if Esteban was a holy person, he would want to stay with the Zuñi. They decided to test him.

They gave him no food or water. At dawn, armed with bows and arrows, they took him outside the pueblo and showed him where the Pima and Papago waited.

Esteban ran.

The Zuñi shot him. As proof he was a man and could be killed, they sent pieces of him to other pueblos.

"If any more like this come, kill them," said the Zuñi. "If you are afraid, ask us and we will kill them."

The Pima and Papago went home. They told the priest Esteban was dead, killed by the Zuñi at Háwikuh.

The priest hurried south. A year later he was back with a band of soldiers led by Francisco Vásquez de Coronado. They asked for corn.

It was planting time, but the Papago traded all the corn they could spare for knives and glass beads. They also sent a warning to the Zuñi.

The war leader took charge at Háwikuh, the Zuñi pueblo the Spaniards would reach first. Rocks were piled on the high terraces. Arrows were prepared, bows checked. Runners were sent to the other five Zuñi pueblos asking for fighting men. Although it was time for rain ceremonies and the fields needed care, hundreds came.

Scouts went to meet the Spaniards. They talked through a trader from the south, a man who knew little of the Zuñi tongue and even less Spanish. They also used signs, which are easily misunderstood.

It was clear the Spaniards were hungry. The scouts said they would return to Háwikuh and ask to have food sent. But the Spaniards were to stay away from Zuñi pueblos.

The Spaniards marched forward. The Zuñi attacked them late one night but were driven off. In the morning,

Pictographs in Canyon de Chelly, Arizona, show mounted Spaniards on the march.

four men met the Spaniards and told them to go away. Two were given little cloaks and sent back to Háwikuh. The other two were kept prisoners. The next day, July 7, 1540, the Spaniards arrived at Háwikuh.

Women, children, old men and boys under fifteen had been sent to caves in a nearby cliff. But the Zuñi were not worried. There were only eighty-five Spaniards on horses and one to two hundred foot soldiers. Most of those were native Americans from Mexico. The Zuñi outnumbered the strangers two to one, and Háwikuh was six stories high with a wall around it.

A hundred Zuñi men met the Spaniards more than a bow shot from the wall. The leader drew a line of sacred corn meal on the ground and warned the Spaniards not to cross it.

Coronado spoke a long time. His words were strange but his tone and manner could be understood. The Spaniards were angry and wanted to go inside the pueblo.

The Zuñi refused.

A priest shouted, then Coronado. The strangers attacked.

The Zuñi fought until their arrows were gone, then retreated to the pueblo. Rocks and arrows were rained on the attackers, especially on Coronado. His gold-plated armor made him an easy target. The Zuñi saw him fall but still the attackers fought. Not only did they fight after their war leader was wounded and carried away, they fought harder!

In an hour it was over. The Zuñi surrendered and asked to join their families in the cliffs. Háwikuh was left to the strangers who looted the storerooms and killed the turkeys kept for feathers. Even the seed corn was taken.

That summer was hard for the Zuñi pueblos. More

strangers kept arriving until there were three hundred Spanish soldiers and eight hundred Mexican native Americans, many with their families, camped outside Háwikuh.

The people had been allowed to return to the pueblo but its storerooms were empty. They had to borrow seed and food from other pueblos and the other pueblos had little to spare. The strangers were always looking for corn, and although they gave presents and talked friendship, they kept stopping the ceremonies. And the fields had to be always guarded against their hungry horses, sheep and cattle.

A group of Spanish soldiers went to northern Arizona to meet the Hopi. They were greeted at the foot of the mesa by the leaders, and a line of sacred corn meal was drawn across the trail. But while the warning not to cross was being given, a horse tried to eat from a basket of corn meal. A Hopi man hit the horse on the nose. The Spaniards attacked.

The battle was short. The Hopi surrendered. But the Spaniards liked that desert even less than the land around Zuñi, so they returned to Háwikuh.

Coronado asked the Zuñi to send messengers to the river pueblos in New Mexico. He wanted their leaders to come to Háwikuh. The Zuñi sent the runners, adding warnings of their own, but the leaders of the river pueblos came to see the strangers for themselves.

They were greeted with presents of cloaks, knives and beads and told to obey a leader far across the ocean, a man whose wisdom they could not know. Then they were given crosses, like prayer sticks but without symbols of paint, feathers and growing things, and told to stop their ceremonies. The leaders said they would talk about it.

From Pecos came Bigotes, the war leader, and Cacique,

Taos pueblo, New Mexico, today

the old and wise leader of that pueblo. Bigotes led a small group of Spanish horsemen and foot soldiers to the Rio Grande pueblos. They visited all of them from south of Albuquerque north to Taos. Everywhere the Spaniards asked for gold. In one pueblo small copper bells were brought out, but they were not what the Spaniards wanted.

At last Bigotes took the Spaniards to Pecos. The pueblo was forty miles east of the Rio Grande at the edge of the plains. Pueblo men passed Pecos on their way to hunt buffalo. Plains people sometimes came to trade or raid and were raided in return.

The Spaniards wanted to see the plains but Bigotes refused to lead them any farther. He and Cacique gave them two young men they had captured years before. One was a Wichita named Sopete, the other a Pawnee the Spaniards called Turk. They were to guide the Spaniards on a short scouting trip.

Bigotes and Cacique knew the two captives wanted to go home. They wouldn't risk escape across the plains alone and unarmed but they would feel safe with the soldiers. If they led the Spaniards far out on the plains and lost them forever, Coronado could not blame the people of Pecos.

Turk saw his chance. Once they were on the plains, he told the Spaniards his people had much gold.

The Spaniards remembered the treasure found in Mexico—the gold jewelry and dishes, the gold-trimmed litter and boat of Montezuma. Did the king of Kansas have all these?

Turk said "yes" to everything. When Sopete said there was no gold in Kansas, Turk told the Spaniards that he had a gold bracelet of his own. When asked to show it, Turk said it was back in Pecos. Bigotes had taken it from him.

The Spaniards rushed back to Pecos. Bigotes and Cacique had never seen a gold bracelet or any gold. The Spaniards did not believe them. All four—Bigotes, old Cacique, Turk and Sopete—were put in chains and taken to Coofor, a pueblo on the Rio Grande, and kept in one of its kivas. When Bigotes and Cacique still said they had never seen a gold bracelet, greyhounds were ordered to attack them.

The pueblos were shocked at this treatment of old and wise leaders and at the use of a sacred kiva for a cage. But they had worse to anger them.

Coronado's expedition, shown in a painting by Frederic Remington

Coronado had moved his troops to the Rio Grande for the winter. There was more feed there for his animals. Because of the cold, he had made the people of Coofor move out so his men could use the pueblo. He sent soldiers up and down the river asking for cotton and rabbit-skin blankets. The men did not wait for the leaders to decide what could be spared. They grabbed the blankets off the old men's backs.

In the pueblos around Coofor, the decision in the kivas was to fight. The men attacked the horse herds first, hoping to put all the strangers on foot. They'd killed only a few horses before the Spaniards rode out to fight.

The Spaniards found the smaller pueblos deserted. The people had gathered in Arenal and Moho, the two strongest pueblos near Coofor.

The war leaders of Arenal had planned well. The roofs

of rooms had been knocked out. The Spaniards could only cross the terraces one way and that way led to a doorway they could only enter one at a time. One at a time the Spaniards were killed until they retreated.

But they did not leave. They knocked holes in the walls of the pueblo's first story and lit smudge fires in the storage rooms. The people in Arenal were smoked out. The battle was over.

The Spaniards tied more than a hundred Arenal warriors to wooden stakes and burned them. Then they burned the roof beams of the pueblo and pulled down the walls.

Moho was stronger, but it had no spring or stream within its walls. The Spaniards camped outside the pueblo and waited for thirst to drive the people out.

Snow saved them once. Then they tried digging a well but its walls fell in before water was reached. It was decided to save the children.

Moho asked for a short truce. All the children were handed over the wall to the Spaniards. They were made slaves.

Three months after the siege began, the last of Moho's people made a night run for the river. Many died in the icy waters and more died from cold after crawling out on the other side. Those who lived became Spanish slaves. Then, to prevent more battles, the Spaniards pulled down eleven pueblos and burned their roof beams.

By planting time the strangers had gone east to the plains. They left Bigotes and Cacique at Pecos but took Turk, Sopete and a Wichita boy named Zabe for guides. Before harvest they were back at Coofor. Zabe had returned with them to Pecos. Sopete had stayed with his people and Turk had been strangled there for lying about the gold.

After another winter at Coofor, the strangers returned to Mexico. They left behind a present of sheep and a priest to teach the pueblo people to be Christians like the Spaniards. Priest and sheep were quickly killed but the memory of Spaniards could not be erased. Nor did the Spaniards forget the Rio Grande pueblos.

SEVEN

Slaves

For almost thirty years, Navahos and Apaches were the pueblos' greatest problem. The wandering bands increased and so did their raids. Travel between pueblos or to sacred lakes became dangerous even for large bands of men. Navahos and Apaches were hated and not to be trusted but they weren't Spaniards. They could be raided in return and then, for a few seasons, there would be peace.

Every ten or fifteen years, a few Spanish soldiers came looking for gold mines in northern Arizona and New Mexico. They found none and were soon gone, but their searching opened an easier road than Coronado had taken. Spaniards began settling along it from Mexico City to the Rio Grande at El Paso. In 1598 they reached the pueblos in northern New Mexico.

Three hundred settlers came with their wagons or belongings and seven thousand animals—horses, cattle and sheep. A hundred soldiers came to guard them and a few priests to build churches and teach native Americans the right way to live.

First they built a town downriver from Coofor, across from the pueblo they called San Juan. But Governor Oñate soon moved his capital north to the mountains, to Santa Fe. From there he sent out soldiers and priests. All pueblos were told to submit to the rule of the Spanish king and become Catholics.

Acoma pueblo, high on a lonely rock, refused to listen. The battle lasted three days. In spite of the sheer cliffs protecting the pueblo, too many of Acoma's men were killed. The pueblo surrendered, sending corn, turkeys and cotton blankets in payment for peace.

The Spaniards refused the payment. All but seventy warriors were killed and thrown off the cliffs. The seventy, along with five hundred women and children, were made slaves. Each man had one foot cut off so he could not run away. Hundreds of the children and women were sent to masters in Mexico City. Two Hopi men who had been visiting Acoma were sent home as a warning. Each had had a hand cut off.

Other pueblos did not refuse to submit. Kings and governors had no meaning for pueblo leaders. How could a man living outside the pueblo decide who farmed what land or take part in the ceremonies?

The soldiers were another matter but perhaps they would give some protection against the Navahos, and if the Spaniards stayed in their towns and behaved, all might be well. As for the priests, their ceremonies could be added to those already held and new kachinas were always welcome.

But the priests wanted the pueblos to give up all their ceremonies. Dances were stopped, the kivas destroyed and ceremonial equipment burned. Leaders were taken to the plazas and whipped until their backs were bloody. The shame was as great as the pain.

It was the beginning of terrible years. Churches were built at the pueblos. At Awatovi the only trees large enough for roof beams grew forty miles away. Hopi men dragged them the forty miles and then up the steep mesa to Awatovi. At Acoma the dirt for the cemetery and church garden was carried up the cliffs one basket at a time.

Luckily there were not enough priests for all the churches. Most pueblos were visited by a priest only once every month or two. These pueblos could hold their ceremonies in secret. But sometimes they were caught and the men hanged or burned at the stake.

Pueblos with full-time churches were places of misery. Mission churches were like villages, each with its own herds, farms, orchards and crafts. "Teaching" native Americans really meant making them do all the work.

Spaniards saw little difference between owning the land and owning the people who lived on it. If governor, settler or soldier needed extra hands, he demanded people from the pueblos. In mission, ranch and town, the native Americans did most of the building, herding, cooking, cleaning, weaving, farming, leatherwork, blacksmithing and digging and tending of irrigation ditches. Cartloads of the food they gathered and the things they made were sent to Mexico City for sale.

It was worse than slavery; not only was the native American working for nothing, each family was also taxed food and cotton cloth. A man had little time left for his own field and weaving.

The only people made happy by the Spaniards were the Navahos. They stole sheep and the women learned to use wool. They stole horses and the men could raid farther and faster. Some Spanish ranches were abandoned because of Navaho raids, but so was Jemez pueblo.

The soldiers chased the Navahos. If they caught any,

the men were killed, the women and children made slaves. But Spanish soldiers could seldom catch Navahos, and when Navahos had captive pueblo women and children to trade, the Spaniards were eager to buy them as slaves.

The pueblos were caught between two enemies. For over sixty years there seemed to be no hope. When a pueblo tried to drive out the Spaniards, it was quickly and bloodily punished. That did not stop another pueblo from trying a few years later. None succeeded. Then Popé began to visit the pueblo leaders.

Popé was a medicine man from San Juan pueblo. He lived at Taos but was seldom there. He spent his days walking from pueblo to pueblo, from Pecos to the Zuñi and Hopi, up and down the Rio Grande. Over and over Popé told the pueblo leaders about his plan to drive out the Spaniards.

All the pueblos would revolt on the same day. It was a simple plan but it took Popé fourteen years to get the pueblo leaders to agree. It was the first and only time the pueblos ever united.

August 13, 1680, was chosen, but someone talked. The Spaniards were warned. Popé moved the attack up three days, and on August 10 every pueblo was awakened by the war cry. Some Navaho bands joined the attack and in three weeks all Spaniards were gone from New Mexico. Four hundred were dead; the rest had fled to El Paso and farther south.

Hundreds of pueblo men had been killed and uncounted hundreds of women and children had been taken as slaves to Mexico by the fleeing Spaniards. But those who remained were free.

They killed chickens, sheep, cattle and Spanish dogs. They cut down fruit trees and burned wheat. All Spanish

The "new" Zuñi pueblo, New Mexico

buildings were torn down. The roof beams of churches were used to rebuild kivas. In every pueblo, ceremonies were held to purify people of everything Spanish.

Soldiers came from Mexico to punish the pueblos but they were only a small band. They destroyed Zia and Santa Ana pueblos and left.

Other enemies remained. The years of raids and Spaniards, from Coronado to the revolt, had drained the pueblos of men. The Zuñis abandoned their six pueblos and moved into one new one they built to the east. Other pueblos had to combine to hold off attacks by Apaches, Navahos and sometimes bands of Utes.

Then, in 1692, Diego de Vargas brought Spanish soldiers and settlers back to Santa Fe. He said he came in peace but people fled the pueblos in terror. Some ran to caves in high cliffs, others to stronger pueblos. Their fear was so great that some took refuge with the hated Navahos and didn't return for fifty years. A group of Tewa fled west to the Hopi. They built their own town, Hano, next to the Hopi pueblos and are still there, speaking their own language, holding their own ceremonies.

Others soon returned to their pueblos. Compared to Oñate and Coronado, de Vargas did come in peace. And when slaves were needed, his soldiers hunted the Navahos. But Navahos couldn't always be found and captured. When soldiers took fourteen Hopi children instead, de Vargas had the soldiers shot or tortured and the children returned.

Even the priests were kinder, and some pueblos let them build churches. Many pueblo people took the new religion. Only the Hopi, except for one town, refused to submit to soldier or church.

The slave church, the Hopi called it, and had only to go to Awatovi to prove it. There were the grooves in the mesa worn by dragging the roof beams for the church. But the people of Awatovi let the priests return. Seventy-five people were baptized.

The leaders of the four other Hopi towns were angered. In 1700 they attacked Awatovi, murdered everyone but a few women and girls and destroyed the town down to the looms and the grinding stones. After that, when priests came to Hopi towns, they were led to the end of Hopi country and told to leave.

The year the Hopi destroyed Awatovi, the Pima and Papago welcomed a priest and his church in the south. Only a few Pima and Papago villages had seen Coronado. For most Pima and Papago, Father Eusebio Francisco Kino was their first contact with the strange men to the south. Instead of soldiers, he brought wheat, melons, cattle, sheep and goats. For a dozen years he traveled back and forth across the desert of southern Arizona.

(Top) The mission church at Rancho de Taos, New Mexico, was begun in 1692 by de Vargas and completed about 1750; (bottom) in Taos pueblo, New Mexico, today, the round ovens in front are still used.

San Xavier del Bac near Tucson, Arizona, which replaced Father Kino's church, as it looked in the 1920's

Most of Father Kino's churches were small brush-roofed shelters, the kind Pimas and Papagos used for cooking. He visited these every few months, baptizing, marrying, burying, tending the sick and giving seeds and animals. At San Xavier and Tumacacori, he taught the Papagos to make mud bricks and they built more permanent churches.

The Papagos were glad to have mud brick walls to shelter behind. Apaches had been forcing them off the mountainsides where they gathered much of their food. The churches offered food and refuge.

But Father Kino died in 1711. The priests who came after him were not so kind and understanding. There were more of them and more work to be done around the missions. People were punished for holding rain-making ceremonies or for tending their own fields instead of working in the church garden or blacksmith shop.

In 1751, Luis Oacpicagua, a Pima, organized a revolt. On November 20, Pimas and Papagos attacked missions and settlements in southern Arizona and northern Mexico.

Most of the priests had been warned and they fled south. The rebels looted San Xavier and killed some loyal Papago families at Tumacacori.

The Spanish governor of the area said the priests had caused the revolt by their cruel treatment of native Americans. But when the priests returned a few weeks later, Pimas and Papagos were living at the missions, waiting to welcome them back. Only a few had taken part in the revolt.

Pimas and Papagos did not like war. They thought killing was a kind of madness. A man who killed an enemy had to spend sixteen days in the desert being purified. But when Pima and Papago men went to war, they seldom lost, even against Apaches.

When Apache raids became too much to bear, they raided back. Usually they destroyed an Apache village. After 1700 they saved the children to sell to Spaniards for slaves. This increased the Apache raids.

A year after the Pima and Papago revolt, soldiers were sent to Tubac to protect the missions. They could do little against the Apaches. By the time the soldiers would reach San Xavier or Tumacacori, the Apaches would be gone. At least once Apaches stole the soldiers' horses out of walled and guarded Tubac.

The seasons passed. Pueblo people, Pimas and Papagos planted their corn and held their ceremonies. Apaches and Navahos raided. Governments changed in Mexico City and everything Spanish became Mexican. In Arizona and New Mexico, the governors changed. So did the flags and the soldiers' uniforms. But Mexican soldiers were no better at catching Apaches and Navahos than the Spanish had been. The raids continued; old hatreds grew stronger.

New strangers in the land were hardly noticed.

EIGHT

Yankees

At first there were only a few. They were strange men who lived like native Americans and were wise in the ways of the plains people. Most were trappers who came to Taos each spring to sell beaver skins, get drunk and fight among themselves. A few were traders who brought wagon trains of goods to Santa Fe and Taos. They were not Spanish or Mexican. Yankees, they were called.

Santa Fe, New Mexico, as it looked in 1841

A pack train on the Santa Fe Trail in the 1820's, shown in a painting by Frederic Remington

Navahos and Apaches watched them closely, especially when half a million dollars' worth of trade goods—guns, cloth, needles, pots and pans, hatchets, knives and iron—began moving from Missouri to Santa Fe every summer. Some of the wagons went on to El Paso but most were too well guarded to risk attacking.

Then, in the summer of 1846, a Yankee army came over the plains from Missouri. Only a few hundred men wore uniforms. The rest looked no different from the traders and trappers.

The United States had declared war on Mexico and the army was coming to take New Mexico, Arizona and California. Pueblo leaders worried about what the Mexican governor would demand of them. The Navahos watched.

As the army neared Santa Fe in the second week of August, all Mexican soldiers fled south. On August 18, the Yankee army marched into Santa Fe and raised a new flag in the plaza. Charles Bent, a trader in Taos, was named governor.

Spanish-Americans with businesses and ranches were

U.S. soldiers in the Mexican-American War (1846–1848), shown in a painting by Frederic Remington

unhappy but there was little change for native Americans. The Yankee army promised to protect the pueblos from Apaches and Navahos and sent out troops to find Navaho bands and sign treaties.

In a few months most of the Yankee army left Santa Fe for Mexico and California. The Spanish-Americans thought it was a good chance to take back the land. They persuaded the leaders of Taos pueblo to join them. On January 19, 1847, Taos warriors and Spanish-Americans attacked the town of Taos. They killed Governor Bent and thirteen others. The governor was scalped while still alive.

Punishment was quick. A troop of Yankee soldiers attacked Taos pueblo, killed a hundred and fifty people and hanged fourteen men. Fifteen Yankees had been killed. It was the last pueblo revolt.

But the Navahos continued to raid.

The Yankees never understood that a Navaho or Apache leader was a leader only as long as people wanted to follow him. If people disagreed with him, they would follow someone else. Seldom did a man lead more than his own small band and any man who wanted to could lead a raiding party.

But when Yankees signed treaties with a dozen Navaho leaders, they thought they bought peace with all Navahos. They really had the friendship of only a few hundred people. The rest of the Navahos continued to raid. In a five-year period in the 1850s, Navahos stole almost half a million sheep, more than thirty thousand cattle, twelve thousand mules and seven thousand horses. Most of the animals had belonged to Yankees.

Yankee ranchers demanded protection. The army built Fort Defiance just south of Canyon de Chelly, Arizona, where many Navahos lived. These bands were often blamed for raids by others. Soldiers were always watching them.

Still the Navahos increased their raids, running off more livestock and killing almost three hundred people in eighteen months. They even attacked Fort Defiance.

Fort Defiance, Arizona, today

In 1863 Colonel Kit Carson was put in charge of "the Navaho problem." He had just rounded up four hundred Mescalero Apaches in New Mexico and put them in Fort Sumner, a hundred and eighty miles southeast of Santa Fe. The rest of the Mescaleros had been killed or had escaped into Mexico. It was hoped he would do even better with the Navahos.

Colonel Carson hired Ute and pueblo warriors to help the army. He asked that the Utes be allowed to keep all captured women and children to sell as slaves in Mexico. The government refused, but it was the only part of his plan they refused.

The plan was to destroy all Navaho food and keep Navahos from escaping anywhere but to the high mountains. All Navaho fields were burned, their sheep, horses and cattle killed or driven away. Thousands of peach trees were cut down so the bark couldn't be eaten during the coming winter. Then Colonel Carson and his men circled in, driving the Navahos deeper into the canyons and mountains. Winter did the rest.

No people had a greater fear of the dead than the Navahos. The frozen bodies piling up around them in their caves probably did more to make them surrender than cold and hunger. A few bands hiding on Black Mesa or in the Grand Canyon never did surrender. But by March those in the mountains, more than eight thousand of them, began to surrender to Colonel Carson.

These weak and starving people were forced to walk three hundred miles to Fort Sumner. The Long Walk, the Navahos call it. They have never forgotten it, Kit Carson or the years spent at Fort Sumner.

With disease, little food and bad water at the fort, hundreds died. And away from home, from the land

Navahos under guard at Fort Sumner, New Mexico, about 1865

woven tight to their myths and ceremonies, even the gods seemed to have left them. They were sick in heart and body.

Let us go home, the leaders begged. Let us go home and we will fight you no more.

After four years they were given some clothes, seeds and farm tools, a few goats and sheep, and allowed to return to the Four Corners area. The few bands that had not surrendered came out of hiding. The Navahos were home. They had only hunger, cold, smallpox, measles, diphtheria and Yankee thieves to worry about.

The Navaho warrior, one of the best American fighting men, was no more. Only the Apache was better. He lasted a little longer.

The Apaches had remained hunters and gatherers of wild food. In hungry times they had raided the Pima and Papago. Without raiding, the Apaches would have starved. But after Spaniards and Mexicans moved into Apache country, there was more to raiding than food.

Navaho men in a hogan on a New Mexico reservation in 1898

Every ranch and village was a storehouse of food, clothing, guns, ammunition, knives, pots, horses, mules and cattle. Raiding Mexicans was better than raiding Pima and Papago and there was much less chance of being caught.

There were never enough Mexican soldiers to hunt down the Apache bands. In 1837 the Mexican government tried to get others to do it by paying $100 for the scalp of an Apache man, $50 for a woman's and $25 for a child's. Some Yankees thought it was easy money.

James Johnson had traded with Apaches around Santa Rita, New Mexico, for years. He invited all the bands around there to a feast. While the Apaches crowded around a pile of trade gifts, Johnson fired small cannon at them. The cannon were loaded with scrap iron, broken glass and old nails. Almost four hundred Apaches were there. Only a few dozen escaped.

The same kind of "feast" was given in other places by other men. At one of them, an Apache medicine man called Geronimo learned to hate Yankees. Before the Mexican government stopped paying for scalps, all Apaches hated Mexicans.

In spite of Johnson and other scalp hunters, Apaches tried to keep peace with the Yankees. Their hatred was for the Mexicans and, besides, raiding was a business. It should be done with as little risk as possible. Yankee wagon trains were larger than Mexican wagons but they were better guarded, and Yankee armies passing through the southwest to California were larger than any since Coronado.

Apaches lived in the canyons where the old Cochise people had farmed. When Yankees came looking for gold, an Apache leader, Mangas Colorado, tried to get rid of them peacefully. He told the gold hunters he would lead them to gold up in Navaho country. The Yankees tied Mangas to a tree and whipped him until he almost died. By the time he healed, another Apache leader, Cochise, had also been turned against Yankees.

Cochise led Apaches living in the Chiricahua Mountains. He was at peace with the Yankees when some Apaches took cattle and a half-Apache boy from a Yankee ranch. United States soldiers did not believe Cochise when he said he didn't have the boy. He offered to try and find the boy, who had been taken by some other band.

The soldiers did not understand that Cochise could not order people even in his own band to do something. He could only persuade, but because he was wise, people listened to him. Even if he discovered where the boy was,

Apache warriors in the late nineteenth century

the Yankee father might not get him back. Among most southwestern tribes, children were believed to belong to the mother's family, not the father's. If the boy's mother's family had taken him, they would feel they had a right to him. (The boy remained with the Apaches and later became Mickey Free, a famous Apache scout for the United States Army.)

The soldiers did not understand any of this. They thought Cochise did not want to give up the men who had made the raid. They made prisoners of Cochise, his wife, his son and three other members of his family. Cochise escaped. He captured three Yankees and tried to trade them for his family. The soldiers hanged three of Cochise's family.

Mangas Colorado was ready to begin his war on Yankees. On July 15, 1862, he joined with Cochise to attack the army at Apache Pass, Arizona. It was the only time Apache bands joined to fight. During the fighting more troops arrived with cannon. The Apaches were driven off. Mangas Colorado was shot and feared to be dying.

His men took him to a Mexican town that had a doctor. If Mangas dies, they said, the town will die, too.

The doctor saved the Apache leader's life but less than a year later, back in his own mountains, Mangas was asked to come to Fort McLane for a peace talk. He was ready for peace. He went and was taken prisoner.

That night General J. R. West told the guards, "That old murderer has gotten away for fifty years. I want him dead or alive in the morning. Do you understand? I want him dead."

During the night, the guards heated their bayonets in the fire and pressed them against Mangas Colorado's bare legs. When the Apache leader rose up, they shot him. In the morning, one soldier scalped him. Another cut off his head and sent it to a museum in the east.

Just as the Apache war was getting started, troops were withdrawn from Arizona and New Mexico to fight the Civil War in the east. Mines and ranches were abandoned because of Apache raids. Only large, heavily guarded wagon trains could get through from Mexico or the east and supplies of all kinds were scarce. By the time the Civil War ended, Yankee and Mexican settlers in southern Arizona and New Mexico were huddled in a few towns and heavily guarded ranches.

The United States government became very concerned, mainly because the winter route to California was across the desert southwest. Mail had to go through and a railroad was being planned. The Apache raids had to be stopped.

Troops poured into southern Arizona and New Mexico but they found no armies or massed groups riding into battle.

Apache war parties, except for the one time at Apache Pass, had no more than thirty or thirty-five men. Some had only six or seven. It was all that was needed. They were experts at planning ambushes, quick raids and clever attacks. They could hide in seemingly flat desert and escape into country where soldiers and horses couldn't follow. Less than a thousand Apache warriors cost the United States thousands of soldiers and hundreds of thousands of dollars.

Yet when Yankees asked for peace talks, Apache leaders usually came. There was no profit in running warfare. Fighting men couldn't take care of their families. To leave them in safety meant taking them into Mexico, away from the canyons, deserts or mountains they belonged to. This separation from home was what brought many to the peace talks. And when Yankees promised them their own land as well as food and clothing, Apaches stopped fighting.

They were put on reservations, tracts of land set aside by the government for native Americans. Agents and soldiers watched over them. But often the reservation was not the land promised, not the Apache band's home, and bands that were not friendly were often put together.

Reservation agents and suppliers made fortunes cheating the government. Apaches were lucky if they received half the food, clothing and blankets they were promised. If men went off the reservation to hunt, they were put in jail. Jail, to a native American, was a death of the spirit.

Cold, hungry and sick with Yankee diseases, Apache bands broke out again and again. They fled to Mexico or tried to hide in their own land, but there were too many Yankee soldiers with Pima and Papago scouts to lead them. General George Crook used Apache scouts from one tribe to hunt escaped bands from another.

Apache leaders died. Men were killed. Bands weakened and surrendered. In September 1886, Geronimo, the last

Apaches at work on an irrigation ditch at San Carlos Indian Agency, Arizona, in 1886

Geronimo and his son (front, third and second from right) and Natchez, son of Cochise (front, center) on their way to Florida in 1886

Apache war leader, and his band of thirty-three people agreed to surrender to General Crook.

A few Apache bands stayed in Mexico and made their last raid on a Mexican village in 1930, but for the United States, the Apache wars were over.

Geronimo's band and almost five hundred other Apaches were sent to prison in Florida, a land so different from their own that they sickened. Some were allowed to live on a reservation in New Mexico and others were taken to Fort Sill, Oklahoma. Geronimo lived there, always asking to be allowed to go home and always refused. None of the last Apache warriors ever saw Arizona again.

NINE

Strangers Still

The battles were over but there was no peace.

When Yankee ranchers wanted grazing land on Apache and Navaho reservations, the good land was exchanged for land not nearly as good.

When silver and copper were found on the San Carlos Apache Reservation in Arizona, the land was taken from the reservation. The mines and town of Globe now belong to Yankees.

When a railroad was built across northern New Mexico and Arizona, the Navaho didn't lose just the land under the tracks. The United States gave the railroad rights to land on each side of the tracks. Some of the strips of land were forty miles deep. The Navahos lost their best springs and much of their best grazing land.

Rivers were dammed for Yankee cities and Yankee ranches. The Pima and Papago reservations lost most of their river water. Wells sunk just outside the reservation borders took their underground water, too.

The surveyor who marked out the Hopi reservation knew nothing about Hopi or Navaho history. He gave the

Pima women preparing corn, using corn stalks as a windbreak

Hopis a neat rectangle in the middle of the Navaho reservation in Arizona. There is no way off except over twenty or thirty miles of Navaho land. Even into the 1900s, Hopis claimed it was dangerous to travel alone and all disappearances were blamed on the Navahos.

The neat rectangle of reservation left one of the Hopi towns on the Navaho reservation and the Navahos claimed land on the Hopi reservation. The government tried to settle the argument by making land on both sides of the border joint land, to be used by both tribes. The arguments have not stopped.

By 1970, Hopis could look down from Oraibi and see Navaho hogans at the foot of the mesa. They protested. The government did nothing. The Hopis said they would get bulldozers and move the Navahos off. The government appointed a committee to study the problem.

The Navahos need the land. Their reservation is three times the size of Massachusetts but it has little water. Grazing is very poor. It takes up to forty acres of land to feed one sheep. The huge reservation can feed thirty to forty thousand people, but there are over a hundred thousand Navahos.

Uranium, oil and coal have been found on the Navaho reservation. This has brought jobs and money to the tribe. It has also brought pollution from electric plants and a strip mine on a mesa that is holy to pueblo people.

Although the Navahos call the land theirs, pueblo people had holy places on it hundreds of years before the Navahos arrived in the desert southwest. It is the cause of much bitterness between pueblo people and Navahos.

Native Americans from the desert southwest fought in World War II. Those who returned from Africa, Europe and the South Pacific told the leaders that schools were needed. Native Americans had to have their own lawyers, doctors, nurses and teachers.

A Hopi kachina-carver, painting an Antelope kachina

At Fort Sumner the Navahos had been promised a school for every thirty children. Now they asked the government to keep that promise. They wanted schools on the reservation where the children could come home often.

Most Indian schools were back east and children would be gone for months or even years. They came back with Yankee ways they could not use on the reservation and without having learned the ceremonies. The ceremonies would die if young people did not learn them. This was true of pueblo as well as Navaho. Both people hid their children in September so they wouldn't be taken.

New schools were built. Most Navahos live in family groups, miles apart, and move each spring and fall with the sheep. Only a few of the children can be bussed each day. But those who must board at school can come home often. And college scholarships have become important items on the tribal budgets.

For years native Americans had no right to vote. And when they were finally allowed to vote, many wouldn't.

Navaho women weaving

A Hopi child watches as a basket is finished.

To register meant signing a paper. When you sign a Yankee paper, they said, the Yankee takes something away from you. But they began to realize that native Americans must also serve in the state senates and the United States government. The Navahos are asking that their two reservations in New Mexico and Arizona be made into a separate Navaho state.

Some things have been given back. Holy places have been returned to some pueblos, land to some tribes and money paid to others for what was taken. But what the government gives, the government can take away.

The government wants to build a dam on a Pima reservation north of Phoenix. It offered the Pimas thirty-one million dollars for the land. The Pimas held an election and voted to refuse the offer. They do not want to move from their land. But the government can condemn the land and take it anyway.

Most native Americans want to live on the reservations. It is their land, their home, their people. But they want good houses, medical care, nearby schools and a decent diet for their children. To have these, they must have jobs, and there are not enough jobs on the reservations. Moving to the cities where the jobs are means losing the old ways and the ties with family and land.

Native Americans of the desert southwest have kept more old ways than most tribes. They have kept their kivas and hogans, their ceremonies and also their old hates and fears. Apaches and Navahos are still strangers to pueblo and Pima and nobody of Spanish or Mexican descent is allowed in Zuñi pueblo because of Coronado. But young people say that must change.

They say all the tribes must unite. They must unite to fight the government.

In 1968, at a gathering of native Americans in Casa Grande, Arizona, an old Navaho said, "There won't be such a thing as Navaho or Hopi. They want something new called Indian."

The old people fear uniting. It is something they have never done, not even to fight the strangers.

But strangers to the desert southwest have always become settlers, have called the land their own and fought to save it.

Index